A TOON BUILT
APO SHENANIGANS

Chris Tait

Edited by
Lisa Nicoll

A TOON BUILT APO SHENANIGANS

Pinocchio:
Once upon a time there was a toon, a toon built apo shenanigans that lay in the north sea as a squeezebox which rose from ancient trestles. People had heard of this toon, far and wide but never knew how to get there. One thing which gave them the key to finding this place - where the piers were chock-a-block with freight, where the toon was ruled by Scrooge, and where there was hope of a better life - was the book written by the mystical hip-hop hero Diablo – a creature who had visited the land and found peace, acceptance but also trouble.
But this story is not about him – it is about you, me, us and them. The ones who are all searching - searching for that better place.
Let me introduce – the butcher, the baker and the candlestick maker.

Conrad:
Hi there, I am Conrad the candlestick maker. I stumbled into candlestick making in childhood and learned my trade by watching a chandler in a window. I often get forgotten with all the torches and lightbulbs flaming but Jack who was nimble and quick did jump over the candlestick supplied by me.

Bailey:
Hello! I am Bailey the Butcher. I have pockets full of pies. I will get up to mischief that will give me

some prospects. Playing practical jokes will let customers share my humour saying they never sausage a place. I camouflage being bashful by telling jokes.

Barnum:	I am Barnum the Baker. I sleep with a recipe book under my pillow so I can bake bread in bed. Sheets are diffused with crumbs. I find it hard to make friends with the other bakers. They think my ingredients are just burnt lumps. I want them to notice me as a real dough puncher.
Pinocchio:	And then there is me, Pinocchio, the gate-keeper of this toon of shenanigans and the teller of this tale. I am a boy with a wooden heart who got his strings cut when I landed here, so I could spread my wings. I made a fiddle with these strings that controlled me so my music could be heard. I danced the Shetland jigs but the woman I loved waltzed away. I have no children and no one to pass on the dances to. I try to help other people's children. If they are struggling, then they copy my jig which cheers them up and they follow the footsteps going back centuries. They join in with friends and eightsome reels take place across the isles. Scrooge gave me the job of gatekeeper to Shenanigans where I can help or hinder new lives. And where I am responsible for placing the Book of Diablo in view of those who may want to journey here.

Bailey: Look what I found in a drawer.

Conrad: Diablo's Book!

Barnum: The key to Pandora's box.

Conrad: To a better life.

Conrad: From the shabby chest of drawers in a back street
                 market stall.

Bailey: It's like what you would read with a lost library
                 ticket.

Barnum: It's out of print.

Conrad: Did they run out of ink half-way?

Bailey: People have searched for this book.

Barnum: For weeks.

Conrad: Months.

Bailey: Years.
                 What does that place-name say?

Conrad: S H E N N

Bailey: S H I N A

Barnum: Shenanigans!

Conrad: The place Diablo went to.
                 The back of beyond.

Barnum: Of what chances are calling our names.

Bailey: Could we be so daring to set foot there.

Bailey: There are pictures of places with smuggled
            goods.

Barnum: Boats and ships are the traffic.

Conrad: Ceilidhs in the halls.

Barnum: Hotels in grand dynasties.

Conrad: Santa delivers the post.

Barnum: They have puffins as pets.

Conrad: Isles are named after whales.

Bailey: That will be Tirvill.

Barnum: Hakki.

Conrad: Haldane.
            We could open the book at random pages.

Barnum: If we learned this information, it could open
            doors.

Conrad: Do you mean to use the book as a door wedge?

Bailey: Or a stepping stone across a stream?

Barnum: It's meant for us to stand on and climb in a
            window to rooms we wouldn't usually have
            access to.

Bailey: This is what I read in the tea leaves.

Conrad: The teachers here treated Diablo like the ugly
            duckling.

Bailey: Always in a pickle.

Conrad: Like me.

Barnum: I heard in bedtime stories about how he did a
            midnight flit to the toon of Shenanigans.

Bailey: He was like a cat among the pigeons.

Barnum: Like me.
            He was born with a virus language like a
            poisoned apple, the perfect fruit to make tarts
            with but that others couldn't understand.

Bailey: Like me.

Barnum: Like me.

Conrad: Like me.

Bailey: The teacher read my marks out in front of the
            class which was fodder for being teased in the
            playground. It was as if I marched up down the
            street with a sandwich board reading dunce.

Conrad: In my school days it was as if the teachers
            announced my marks like news headlines.
            People were invited to hear them being read out
            as an audience. My scrapes and failures were

plastered on every wall and newspaper for miles.
All the other children with high marks were
knighted on thrones in higher lasses. Their
universities gleamed welcoming them like
palaces and job prospects beckoned them like
gold gloves.
I had no study or job options in any nook or
cranny but to play with my candlesticks which
gave a light like a chandelier though people just
looked down their noses at.

Barnum: From childhood I read recipes which trailed over
the floor the more I threw in the pots and pans
and the more I stirred in all directions. Raisins
and currants flew as storms with puddles of milk
and water. The bread and cakes swelled and
climbed onto tiers.
I had customers but their orders were as if the
pots and pans were outside of my reach, the
ingredients couldn't be ordered because they
were in a faraway land and couldn't arrive in
time and the produce rotted because I thought
health and safety was an old wives' tales.
My recipe book is like the bible which reads like
'*hubble bubble, toil and trouble*'.

Conrad: Here my premises are dismissed as hazardous.

Bailey: Here my books don't balance when I weigh them.

Barnum: Here my bakery is accused of being a sardine tin.

Conrad: We have to go to this toon they call Shenanigans.

Bailey: Follow in Diablo's footsteps.

Barnum: Find others who speak our language.

Bailey: Are we going from the frying pan into the fire?

Barnum: I knead the dough.

Conrad: I need a thermometer.

Bailey: I need a carving knife.

Conrad: Our topsy turvy houses here are built by three little pigs.

Bailey: With bent nails and screws.

Conrad: We are cows in bunk beds here.

Bailey: We disrupt and interrupt neighbours.

Barnum: Then all trip and tumble.

Conrad: Bumble and stumble.

Bailey: And all fall down.

Beat

Pinocchio: Bailey the butcher, Barnum the baker and Conrad the candlestick maker will sail to the toon but as they can't afford the fare then they will have to

hitchhike or be stowaways to cross the stormy
seas.

Conrad: Our trip will be in a tub which we will borrow
and beg.

Bailey: I will bundle the tub with enough clobber to feed
us.

Barnum: I will bake on route.

Conrad: On a basin of gravy.

Bailey: In gale force winds.

Conrad: My light will show us red herrings in the mist.

Bailey: Which will take us to rocks and nets of
Shenanigans.

Barnum: My compass readings will transport us back to
the shore.

Conrad: The wooden spoon will be our oar. I will row
anti-clockwise.

Bailey: The lamb chop will be a good anchor. I have one
in my shop.

Conrad: It's like plunging out a window.

Barnum: Parachuting into a cabbage patch.

Conrad: Or in the middle of a maze garden.

Bailey:	If we stay here some hag will jinx us for the rest of our time here.

Barnum:	Or we will smash a mirror.

Conrad:	Or tear a spider's web.

Bailey:	So we should fill our bags with four leaf clovers.

Barnum:	Snap a wish bone.

Conrad:	And set sail.

| Pinocchio: | They will travel to the toon built apo shenanigans and agitate people. They will make conversation about their butchers, bakers and candlestick makers until people are sick of it and avoid them. |

They will outstay their welcome and trespass. Bailey the butcher will be a lamb to the slaughter. Barnum the baker will have his fingers in pies. Conrad the candlestick maker's chandlery will be a shambles.

Beat

Bailey:	I found this gravy boat in a back yard.

Barnum:	You shouldn't have touched it.

Conrad:	We could fix it up.

Bailey:	Give it a good scrub.

Barnum: It looks like it has been in a sea battle.

Conrad: A wreck dragged from the sea bed.

Bailey: It is a Viking re-enactment.

Barnum: It appears totally un-sea worthy.

Conrad: We will arrive like Norse raiders.

Bailey: I read in the bible about building Noah's ark.

Barnum: We should take tins of soup.

Conrad: Aprons.

Barnum: The sail post is a mop.

Conrad: There isn't enough room for one of us, never mind three.

Bailey: Shoehorn us in.

Barnum: I feel less and less safe.

Conrad: We are wobbling about.

Bailey: To sea!

Beat

Bailey: The rain is doing a day shift, and a night shift.

Barnum: The wind is puffing.

Conrad: The sleet is hypnotising. The waves are high.

Bailey: The gravy boat might tip.

Conrad: Lower the lamb chop anchor.

Barnum: I cannot see.

Bailey: Light the candle.

Barnum: Why are the birds angry at my bread crumbs?

Bailey: They know we are coming.

Barnum: I sent a message in a bottle to the village.

Conrad: Their reply was a map, saying, when we arrive,
               we must climb cliffs.

Barnum: I don't like heights.

Bailey: They say we can stay at outbuildings that look
               preyed upon.

Barnum: They say we will be staying in what looks like
               sheep pens.

Conrad: I feel like a rabbit in the headlights.

Bailey: That is your demeanour.

Barnum: A lost lamb.

Conrad: I am a crooked man.

Bailey: Who walked a crooked mile.

Barnum: And found a crooked sixpence.

Conrad: Upon a crooked style.

Barnum: I have nightmares that we will get off on the
                 wrong foot.

Conrad: With no cobbler.

Bailey: It's such a big step to take.

Barnum: We will need giant's shoes.

Conrad: Will the town stock those?

Pinocchio: I am Pinocchio, the gate-keeper of this Toon.
                 There are myths and legends which can be traced
                 back to the Norse creation myths. I turned those
                 tales on their head. It makes very entertaining
                 storytelling for tourists.
                 The opportunities include fishing with the
                 stalwart boats, crofting with hardy sheep,
                 knitting which sells across the world and the
                 locals who are very welcoming.
                 However, there can be very uncompromising
                 weather, it's tricky to get a job and there is a
                 limited range of shops.
                 I make sure that intruders have something
                 substantial to offer to cross the Billy Goat's Gruff
                 bridge and into this place.

Conrad: We can provide references.

Pinocchio: Who from, Neptune?

Conrad: Pirates. We sailed the Bermuda triangle.

Pinocchio:	In a paper boat?

Bailey:	No. In a gravy boat.

Conrad:	Stranded, adrift and back to square one.

Pinocchio:	Did you dwell in the belly of a whale?

Conrad:	Yes indeed.

Pinocchio:	That is quite a trip in a tub.

Beat

	Who is this in the butcher's aprons?

Bailey:	I am Bailey the Butcher.

Pinocchio:	Who is this in the baker's hat?

Barnum:	I am Barnum The Baker.

Pinocchio:	Who is this bundled with candlesticks?

Conrad:	I am Conrad The Candlestick maker.

Pinocchio:	So Bailey the butcher, what can you bring to the toon?

Bailey:	I didn't know how to write a warning sign when the floors were wet, so wagged my finger, pointed to the floor and looked sad.

Pinocchio:	Charades.

13

Bailey: That is the apprenticeship I had.

Pinocchio: Tell me more.

Bailey: I had to take steps to prevent the build-up of ice
                   on the floors, so did folk dance steps while the
                   customers responded by slipping.

Pinocchio: That is very dangerous.

Bailey: The fridge shivered so I draped it with a blanket.

Pinocchio: Can you think of a reason why this town should
                   employ you?

Bailey: I did get orders wrong but now count on my
                   fingers. 10, 9, 8, 7, 6, 5, 4, 3, 2, 1.
                   My shelves are stacked with sausages, pies, beef
                   and lamb which customers laugh at for being
                   past its sell-by date. So I pack them with even
                   more old meat and they laugh even louder. I have
                   a great store of jokes from Christmas crackers.
                   There would be never a dull moment with me as
                   a butcher.

Pinocchio: Sells out-of-date meat.
                   Can't count.
                   Tells jokes.

Pinocchio: So Barnum the baker what can you bring to the
                   town?

Barnum: My boss was a tyrant who should have been
                   raked over coals.

Pinocchio: He is a good friend of mine.

Barnum: He told me I didn't add a key ingredient, but you
                 can't put keys in bread.

Pinocchio: What was the missing ingredient?

Barnum: Flour.
                 He said I didn't know what my oven needs, well it
                 can't speak.

Pinocchio: Can you work an oven?

Barnum: I give it a slap.

Pinocchio: What more baking experience do you have?

Barnum: My boss said I didn't follow the recipe, well I can't
                 walk behind it.

Pinocchio: Can you think of a reason why this town should
                 employ you?

Barnum: Sometimes I forgot to preheat the oven but have
                 learned my lesson and set it to a furnace.
                 I didn't measure the ingredients correctly so try
                 to keep score.
                 I open the oven door too much so handcuff
                 myself to the handle.
                 At times my cakes are too dry or wet or the
                 wrong temperature so check the weather
                 forecast.

Pinocchio: Slaps Ovens.
               Cannot follow recipes.
               Doesn't measure ingredients.

Pinocchio: So, Conrad the candlestick maker what can you
               bring to the town?

Conrad: I don't wear goggles so wax splashes in my eyes
               and I make mistakes.

Pinocchio: Expand on your practice.

Conrad: I work barefoot and wear loose clothes near
               flames getting scalded and burned.

Pinocchio: Protective clothing is company policy.

Conrad: Water made the wax splatter causing a bigger
               splash.

Pinocchio: What a clutter.

Conrad: I used up the first aid kit.

Pinocchio: So you didn't use appropriate equipment or
               materials.

Conrad: I left the workspace unattended as an invitation
               for animals to sneak in, prowl around and leave a
               huge mess.

Pinocchio: A circus!

Conrad: Flammable materials weren't cleared and were
               scattered as tokens.

Pinocchio: Can you think of a reason why this town should
                employ you?

Conrad: I am good at creating fire hazards.
                I can make candles from ear wax.
                I am very helpful for example I helped Little Bo
                Peep when she lost her sheep.
                I let my disadvantages spur me on.

Pinocchio: Works barefoot.
                No first aid kit.
                Good at creating fire hazards.

Beat

                And what can you tell me about the textbook?

Bailey: Diablo's book?

Pinocchio: What draws you to it?

Barnum: It's written like disruptive messages.

Pinocchio: A virus language.

Conrad: It reads like voices trapped in my head.

Bailey: The book is a tour guide of the toon built apo
                shenanigans.

Barnum: It tells of castles.

Conrad: Viking settlements.

Bailey: The capital.

Conrad: A mediaeval circus.

Bailey: It's written like shuffled cards with sleight of
               hand.

Barnum: Characters lurk in the shadows.

Bailey: Bits of text ping out.

Barnum: Some vanish.

Conrad: Then no-one can find them.

Bailey: It's written as if the author chose random lines.

Barnum: Scrolled up and down the page.

Conrad: Repeated words with the same letter like hip hop.

Bailey: That I could read.

Barnum: That I could understand.

Conrad: Not many people understand us.

Pinocchio: Okay, I have heard enough, the town shall be in
               touch with a decision if you have the right skills
               to enter this place.

                        Beat

Dear Bailey, on behalf of the toon of shenanigans
we will not be employing you as butcher.

The reason is you will struggle with numbers such as addition and subtraction. You will find taking orders and messages a hurdle. You will grapple with telling the time.

Dear Barnum, on behalf of the toon of shenanigans we will not be employing you as baker. The reason is because you appear shell shocked. You have traits which could hamper your performance. You may be prone to meltdowns.

Dear Conrad, on behalf of the toon of shenanigans we will not be employing you as candlestick maker. The reason is because you appear to be very distracted. Your handwriting is very messy. You have issues with balance.

Conrad:	We came here because they put me down, criticised my every fault, belittled me to other people, used work and money as a weapon to punish me with and always made me feel second best.
Barnum:	Where I am from is like being on a train but with no driver. I wasn't supervised with secure doors so the passengers were shifty.
Conrad:	There was no help or advice.
Bailey:	I worried people like me got sent away on witch hunts or to institutions.

Barnum: I fended myself from threats, an acid tongue and harsh words by quickly putting up defences.

Conrad: I thought the police rounded people up, then gave them treatments to be normal.

Bailey: Always given reasons to feel ashamed, foolish and to apologise over and over.

Barnum: Intimidated to become timid and fearful so that even small things would hunt me.

Conrad: Isolating me, cutting me off from other people and manipulating me to know who they want.

Bailey: Staring at me like I am unstable then discussing my faults in depth saying I gave them no peace. They were stuck in a rut.

Barnum: They rummaged in all my drawers and cupboards and told my private business.

Bailey: We thought coming here you would understand us.

Conrad: Give us opportunities.

Barnum: Like Diablo.

Conrad: I can't read or write and find it very difficult to get chances.

Bailey: No compliments, praise, acknowledgement or stimulating conversation just scathing.

Barnum: Teachers made sure there was no light at the end of my tunnel.

Conrad: Punishments were so hard and carried on for weeks

Bailey: I had to listen to dictation and speeches to make me more conventional.

Barnum: They would tell me that I was a source of gossip and that people were puzzled about me. That people could sense tension. That I was immature and hogged attention.

Conrad: While they made other people and their achievements seem worthy of prizes and medals.

Bailey: They got people to gang up against me and force me to be something I wasn't. I was nagged to apologise and compensate for things I hadn't done.

Conrad: We broke the mould.

Barnum: We had to for safety reasons.

Pinocchio: I have listened to your stories and crammed them in. You are an endangered crowd matching my bygone experience. You require careful instructions as I once did with dance steps. You could falter into the rhythm of the town each with your own pulse. So I recommended finding a place to hide and tell no-one your address.

Hide from Scrooge because he will hound you like a noxious cat and mouse game. Camouflage and disguise yourselves. Enter into this toon of shenanigans. But be cautious.

Barnum: We have struck hell's door knocker.

Bailey: With our skeletal hands.

Conrad: This place is bubonic.

Barnum: To get work you must be bionic.

Conrad: Street names are puns.

Bailey: Hansel and Gretel are neighbours.

Barnum: Mother Hubbard's cupboard is jammed ready to burst.

Conrad: A toon built apo shenanigans.

Bailey: Cats in cradles.

Barnum: Pubs are ten green bottles.

Conrad: An Aladdin's cave of poisons.

Bailey: There are signs that don't make sense.

Barnum: A lady with a lollypop stopped traffic.

Conrad: So if she used a toffee apple would the traffic stick?

Bailey: Traffic lights with a green man so he must be the leprechaun.

Barnum: That red man will be the devil.

Conrad: The cars move like bats out of hell.

Bailey: Signs point to old sandcastles.

Barnum: Dug with a bucket and spade.

Conrad: The streets are paved with mould.

Bailey: Should that not be gold?
               People stare at us like they are looking through a telescope.

Barnum: Maybe reading our star signs. A toon built apo shenanigans.

Bailey: All these funny noises.

Barnum: Tractors jolting along.

Conrad: Sheep blathering.

Bailey: Fish babbling.

Barnum: Hens and ducks haggling.

Conrad: Ship's horns droning.

Bailey: Bucking broncos moaning.
               I can't tune into the noise.

Barnum: I feel over stimulated.

Conrad: I need to curl into a shell.

Bailey: I want to hibernate.

Barnum: I want to stick something in my ears.

Conrad: The people are hustling and bustling.

Bailey: On and off boats.

Barnum: Round and round farms like vicious circles.

Conrad: Dialects of grumbles and grunts.

Bailey: Illegitimate Jack and Jill.

Conrad: Brawling in pubs.

Barnum: Scuffles and tussles.

Bailey: People are looking at us like we have three heads.

Barnum: They could be reading our palms.

Conrad: Crystal gazing.

Bailey: Three spirits gave predictions.

Conrad: We will always have notoriety.

Barnum: Unrestrained disorder.

Bailey: Tumult and torment.

Barnum: We have gotten a rat's reception.

Conrad: A toon built apo shenanigans.

Barnum: We will be deported.

Bailey: We have no passports but mugshots.

Conrad: We did midnight flits so have no proof of address.

Bailey: Where will we live?

Conrad: We knocked on every door for miles.

Barnum: Left a trail of breadcrumbs to find our way back.

Bailey: There was no room at the inn.

Bailey: We knocked on doors.

Barnum: Camped on employer's doorsteps.

Conrad: But they tripped over us.

Bailey: Threw buckets of water on us.

Barnum: That is how we washed.

Bailey: I posted chops in their letterbox.

Barnum: I baked from the bucket with a hole.

Conrad: I posed holding a candle stick in their window.

Bailey: Some of the doors we knocked on were sheds where we trod on plants.

Barnum: The only welcome was by a rogue with a wonky door handle.

Conrad: Stables where the cowboy charged at us on
               horseback.

Barnum: Snoozing and snoring.

Conrad: Cottages, croft houses and cats in cradles.

Bailey: We could bunk at the barn.

Barnum: Do we get the key from a cow?

Conrad: We could squeeze through the cat flap.

Bailey: I'm not going through that.

Conrad: Bailey you first.

Bailey: Me?

Conrad: Yes.

Bailey: This is like being swallowed.

Barnum: I'm stuck.

Conrad: I will limbo under a crack.

Bailey: I feel as if I am in an envelope.

Barnum: It is so cramped in here

Conrad: It's as if we are being chewed.

Bailey: Pretend we are holding a barn dance.

Barnum: Who would dance here?

Conrad: As a housewarming because I'm becoming a snowman.

Barnum: Warm your hands with my oven gloves.

Conrad: Loose floorboards for us to spin on.

Bailey: Splintered rafters nearly dropping the building.

Conrad: Knocks on the bashed door provide a beat.

Bailey: Is that music from next door's pub?

Barnum: Pinocchio should teach us his dances.

Conrad: Where is he?

Bailey: He has left us to dance alone.

Barnum: I would rather be in a tent away from these totem poles of creepy crawlies.

Conrad: I think people could spy on us through these chinks.

Bailey: We could guard the chinks.

Barnum: While we hatch a plan to make money.

Conrad: We must go to market. Sell what we have.

Bailey: I have no meat to sell.

Barnum: I have no flour to bake bread.

Conrad: I have no wax to make candles.

Pinocchio: Goldilocks threw all her belongings out the window. Goldilocks and Dick Whittington have separated. They each wanted half of everything. A doll landed on my head. A toy train struck me like a skittle. A toy soldier marched past me. This could be your stock for the stalls. Even though it's damaged.
Scars show character.

Barnum: Roll up, roll up, come and get your toys.

Bailey: A chess set where all of the pieces play against each other.

Conrad: They throw each other off the board.

Barnum: They stand on squares which they aren't supposed to.

Bailey: They take shortcuts.

Conrad: They block each other.

Barnum: Here we have a teddy bear with an invite to a picnic.

Bailey: Perhaps the mad hatter's tea party.

Conrad: He will gobble up cake.

Barnum: Make his fur sticky.

Bailey: Why is no-one buying?

Pinocchio: People are scorning your products.

Barnum: No one knows they are from a skip.

Conrad: Or a car boot sale.

Pinocchio: Dick Whittington and Goldilocks' tantrums left
                            the house in a shell. These objects are weapons
                            and trophies from their battles.

Bailey: They are looking at us up and down.

Barnum: They are listening to our conversation.

Conrad: Let's give them something to talk about.

Bailey: I thought the people would understand us.

Barnum: They need a tour guide for our language.

Conrad: It's as if we have our own made-up alphabet.

Bailey: They are staring at us like we are from another
                            planet.

Pinocchio: The customers are getting bored.

Bailey: We could lullaby them.

Bailey, Barnum,
Conrad and
Pinocchio: Row, row, row your boat gently down the stream
                            Merrily, merrily, merrily life is but a dream.

Pinocchio: Scrooge - run!

Beat

Barnum: People were told not to buy from us.

Conrad: They are fussy saying that the goods have bits
                    missing.

Bailey: They don't work.

Barnum: That they are faulty.

Conrad: Like us.

Bailey: Like us.

Barnum: Like us.

Pinocchio: That's not true. My strings were cut and I still
                    work.

Bailey: We need to eat. We need people to buy from us.

Pinocchio: I have secret information about Old Mother
                    Hubbard's cupboard.

Bailey: Tell us more.

Pinocchio: I was sworn to secrecy but it holds groceries fit
                    for a banquet. Her husband Scrooge has grand
                    friends who they dine with so store three courses
                    for Old King Cole. You could steal from Old
                    Mother Hubbard's cupboard.

Bailey: Old mother Hubbard has nightmares about her cupboard being bare.

Barnum: I hear her screaming in the night about a misplaced salt pot.

Pinocchio: She festoons the cupboard with food.

Barnum: What would happen if someone took an item from her cupboard?

Pinocchio: I was once found guilty of stealing and punished with a penalty of scrubbing the silverware. Whenever I visit there then I get my bag searched and am warned to take no food off the premises. She memorises the stock as if it's the holy grail. Her food is cooked by recipes handed down for generations and with handmade ingredients. You can't access the cupboard unless you know the password. It is locked with several keys. Which she guards.
She has servants who are each responsible for certain shelves. However, I could distract her by asking to hear the story of her fret. She loves to tell that story.
When Hubbard isn't looking then you could sneak in. While in conversation with me, you will clear the shelves.

Bailey: Once inside we could pickpocket grapes.

Conrad: Grab handfuls of ham.

Barnum: Tablespoons of flour.

Conrad: Ounces of oranges and lemons.

Bailey: We could slip in and with sleight of hand and fill
               our apron.

Conrad: One of us could try to sell her wares.

Bailey: Her nightmare would come true of the cupboard
               being bare.

Conrad: We must take the chance.

Barnum: I need the food.

Bailey: I need the money.

Conrad: What a plan!

Beat

Bailey: Roll up, roll up for your milk fresh from the cow
               which jumped over the moon.

Barnum: Come and get your bread, it's a labour of loaf.

Conrad: Here are your eggs for an egg and spoon race.

Bailey: The moon is made of cheese and please sample
               some from here.

Barnum: Good morning, PC Pilchard, here is a
               smorgasbord on offer for you.

PC Pilchard: Old Mother Hubbard screamed like opera about the missing cupboard items.

Conrad: If we are aware of those errands we will indeed inform you.

PC Pilchard: I am arresting you three for the theft of nibbles from Old Mother Hubbard's cupboard.

Bailey: You have no proof.

PC Pilchard: Your sticky fingerprints are all over the cupboard.
Barnum, your syrupy footsteps can be traced from there to here.
Conrad, you dropped crumbs between locations which creatures tailed you for.
Do you have a licence?

Bailey: What is a licence?

PC Pilchard: You need a licence to sell on the street.

Pinocchio: A thumbs up saying you can do something.

Conrad: What if the thumb points down.

Pinocchio: It means you are naughty.

Barnum: So you can be a jester every day!

Conrad: That's a funny rule.

PC Pilchard: You do not have the right to sell here.

Bailey: I have permission for pranks.

PC Pilchard: You will each be fined.

Conrad: My piggy bank is empty.

PC Pilchard: You will be deported on the gravy boat you sailed in on.

Conrad: We have no boat.

Barnum: It sailed off to sea.

PC Pilchard: You shall have to swim then. If you cannot pay up.

Bailey: How will we pay?

Pinocchio: I encouraged them to copy Robin Hood but only because they are fending for themselves.

PC Pilchard: Someone who has already corrupted the court of justice with lies should obey the law.

Pinocchio: I didn't mean to stir the hornet's nest.

PC Pilchard: Pinocchio, you let them past the gate of this toon, so I am leaving you responsible for repaying the money within the week.

Pinocchio: I can't dance enough in that time to foot the bill.

PC Pilchard: Choreograph that between yourselves.

Bailey: Pinocchio, could you teach us how to dance the eightsome reel?

Barnum: We could all dance together.

Conrad: So we can make more money.

Pinocchio: Bailey - stand in the middle and skip around in a ring.

Barnum: Like ring-a-ring-a roses.

Pinocchio: Much faster than that and you don't all fall down.

Conrad: I can't leap around like this.

Pinocchio: Once you have rung 16 times then ladies dance right-hand across with partners on their left side.

Bailey: I can't count.

Barnum: I guess and make it up.

Barnum: How will we ever make money from this.

Conrad: People will laugh at the spectacle.

Pinocchio: Then change to men dancing left-hand across in centre back.

Barnum: It takes time for me to process.

Bailey: It takes me longer.

Conrad: I feel like a haggis being tossed as a grenade.

Bailey: You are all out of tune.

Barnum: This is a scrum.

Conrad: I can't juggle two things at once.

Pinocchio: Pick it up from skipping round in a ring again.

Barnum: I will stand in the middle because I feel like a
                   dumpling.

Bailey: You dance like one too.

Conrad: I have to whirl with partners which makes me
                   feel seasick.

Pinocchio: You are not going to make any money at this rate.

Bailey: Once we have practised then we can raise the
                   rates.

Barnum: I quit.

Beat

Pinocchio: You could break into the bank.

Bailey: Around this strip?

Barnum: I am not robbing a bank.

Conrad: Why are you a coward?

Pinocchio: You mastered Hubbard's cupboard so her other
                   half's must be a doddle.

Bailey: Scrooge and Hubbard are married?

Pinocchio: Yes. They rule the toon.
                 They were the ones that cut my strings.

Bailey: How will we rob the bank?

Barnum: I have butter fingers.

Pinocchio: Look at Diablo's book it has the instructions.

Conrad: The layout of the sewer.

Bailey: Squiggly pipes.

Barnum: The architecture of Scrooge's bank.

Conrad: Customer's names and addresses.

Bailey: Who were born with a silver spoon in their
                 mouth.

Pinocchio: Diablo gives clear instructions.

Conrad: Travel in the night like highwaymen.

Conrad: Prize open a manhole.

Bailey: Enter like an escape artist.

Barnum: Squeeze through the sewer tunnel.

Conrad: The winding underpass.

Bailey: Poke bricks out with a broom.

Barnum: Unpick locks.

Conrad: Hack.

Bailey: A lucky dip.

Barnum: Slip pounds and notes, up sleeves, as magic
               tricks.

Conrad: Bailey, you are reading it backwards.

Bailey: We will climb up the tube and through the grate.

Barnum: Dressed like the monopoly man.

Conrad: A cleaner.

Bailey: Get clothes from the laundry basket.

Pinocchio: The instructions were Diablo's course criteria.
               The sewer layout is the college he went to.
               Pipes are the channels he took where he was
               warned not to return to.

Conrad: We will follow Diablo's path.

Bailey: Will we return?

Beat

Bailey: The sewer is welcoming.

Pinocchio: I'll stand guard.

Barnum: It is a septic tank.

38

Pinocchio: Pick the lock with a needle.

Conrad: It's picked.

Pinocchio: Smash the piggy bank with an axe.

Barnum: The piggy bank?

Pinocchio: The safe.

Bailey: The safe code is a ouija board.

Barnum: Chip the safe with a chisel-like a block of cheese.

Conrad: Disguise the alarm as a nightclub noise.

Bailey: Jam anti-theft devices with a spoon.

Bailey: Pinocchio, what is the code?

Pinocchio: One, two, three, four, five once I caught a fish alive.

Barnum: One, two, three, four, five.

Conrad: Tap it in quick.

Bailey: Look at all that bling.

Barnum: Hump bags of coins in the toilet.

Conrad: Swallow notes up in a hoover.

Conrad: It's as if we are retrieving Aladdin's lamp.

Bailey: Snatch it all.

Barnum: Leave some for me.

Conrad: Me too.

Bailey: I want the crown jewels.

Barnum: I blew a wish for the diamonds.

Conrad: I want the gold!

Bailey: What's that noise?

Barnum: It's dancing in my head.

Conrad: It's singing in my ears.

Pinocchio: The alarm! Climb back up the pipes

Beat

Scrooge: Ladies and gentlemen, I Scrooge, welcome you all
                today for the case which is Bailey the butcher,
                Barnum the baker and Conrad the candlestick
                maker who stand accused of the robbing of my
                bank. Since their arrival here the town has been
                turned upside down between them breaking into
                buildings, squatting and all manner of
                foolishness. I have had complaints from a
                variety of residents at how they have
                encountered problems from them including
                extra work for the police. There is no witness
                statement or documents which can prove
                otherwise.

40

They have dragged Pinocchio into their nonsense which has in turn had repercussions for him. I hope you can join me in my decision to get them to leave once and for all.

Barnum: Scrooge you are a big bully.

Conrad: A coward in disguise.

Bailey: A dictator.

Scrooge: Order in court.

Bailey: I feel so lonely in this town.

Barnum: Like nobody's child.

Conrad: I am always left out.

Bailey: We took a huge risk by coming here.

Barnum: It was a gamble to tear up our routes.

Conrad: Take a perilous voyage.

Bailey: To come here with no welcome.

Barnum: To be lured into trouble.

Bailey: Our only source of wisdom was Diablo's book.

Scrooge: Said by someone who can't read!

Barnum: We left our friends and family.

Conrad: Because we were stuck in a rut.

Bailey: We thought this would maybe give us prospects.

Barnum: So we departed our briar patch.

Conrad: The book was like a map.

Pinocchio: My parents Scrooge and Old Mother Hubbard
                     always put me on trial.

Conrad: Scrooge is your dad?

Barnum: Mother Hubbard is your mum?

Bailey, Barnum,
and Conrad: They cut your strings?!

Scrooge: I thought cutting his strings and restricting him
                     would make him more normal. I disowned him
                     because I was embarrassed about the way he was
                     and the things he did. I couldn't pass on my
                     throne to him because the toon would be even
                     more chaotic than it is now.

Pinocchio: You put me down and slagged me off, slagged me
                     off to other people, used work and money as a
                     weapon to punish me with and always made me
                     feel ignored.

Scrooge: Well what use were you? I need a proper boy to
                     take over my kingdom.

Pinocchio: It begun with Diablo who was a very intelligent
                     lad, but you drove him away because his way
                     with words was unconventional.

I understood him though.
Bailey's misunderstanding of numbers and
letters is what you made sure the town laughed
at him about. You didn't explain the traits, so
they misunderstand him.
For Barnum you did the same. He can't get the
chance to practise as a baker as you tell them
they are a loner, vulnerable, odd, memorises
nonsense and worships a recipe book.
With Conrad, you just said he was away with the
fairies. The painstaking work he is more than
capable of which could light the town and add a
lovely touch to special occasions has been
dismissed.
They should be given suitable opportunities.
If they were given the right support then they
would excel in their careers. Instead of being
laughed at mocked and ridiculed.
The toon could gain from their service.

Scrooge: I have seen this toon sink.

Pinocchio: It's sinking now.

Barnum: I have no more corners to turn.

Conrad: I cannot justify it anymore.

Bailey: I question myself.

Pinocchio: Dad, what do you have to say for yourself.
                You have treated people who you say are

different unfairly and kept quiet about the bullying they experience.

Bailey: I feel so daunted about returning to work.

Barnum: The challenges of managing tasks.

Conrad: Impatient customers.

Bailey: Getting on with staff.

Barnum: Finding my way round buildings.

Conrad: Concentrating with vague instructions.

Barnum: I plead for help Mr Scrooge.

Bailey: Help to understand the numbers.

Conrad: The words.

Bailey: The sounds.

Scrooge: There are places which cater for you.

Pinocchio: You listened to only the negative things said about them and made it into folklore.
                You put them in situations which were very damaging to their welfare.

Scrooge: Such as?

Pinocchio: Workplaces where they were forced to sell dodgy goods for commission. With cliques of people who bull baited them.

Provided them with very little instruction.
They have nowhere to live but the margins of the
town to escape you. You could transfer the funds
wasted on the rich and share it with these three.

Scrooge: I shall do no such thing!

Pinocchio: I shall tell everyone the truth.

Scrooge: They will never believe you Pinocchio. You tell
                lies.

Pinocchio: Since you cut my strings, I tell the truth. Look
                through the floorboard at your Christmases past.

Scrooge: As a child I read books about treasure so I could
                be a toff.

Pinocchio: Look in the window at your Christmas present.

Scrooge: The toon is laughing at me.
                They are doing impersonations!
                No one is cheering me.

Bailey: That's how it feels to be me.

Conrad: Folk laughing, mocking.

Barnum: Not backing you.

Pinocchio: Look in the mirror at your Christmases yet to
                come.

Bailey: I see us having to join elves as partners in crime
                to survive.

Barnum: Jailed on Christmas day.

Conrad: With only snowmen as cell mates.

Pinocchio: As community service, you slave in the markets.

Bailey: For pittance.

Barnum: Freeze in a hovel.

Conrad: Ration pecks of food.

Pinocchio: Scrooge it is you that is on trial.
                   Bailey the butcher, Barnum the baker, Conrad the
                   candlestick maker - you should decide the fate of
                   my father.

Bailey: In the vault there was a sacred page.

Barnum: It was ripped from Diablo's book.

Conrad: It was made to look like litter.

Bailey: Every other page was immaculate as if done by a
                   scribe.

Conrad: It was shoved in the corner.

Barnum: It said that Diablo deciphered that the town was
                   supposed to be ruled by a boy born of strings.

Bailey: A leader who was string born shall overthrow the
                   town it said.

Scrooge: None of you can read.

Barnum: Diablo's book makes perfect sense to us.

Scrooge: Pinocchio, I gave you the responsibility as gate-
               keeper to stop people like this entering the town
               who spout such rubbish.

Bailey: Did you rip the page Scrooge?

Scrooge: You all talk gobbledygook. Just like that book.

Pinocchio: You cut my strings like an umbilical cord when I
               was six.

Scrooge: I couldn't have a puppet boy as a leader.

Pinocchio: It says on this page puppets are supposed to be
               leaders.

Scrooge: Myself and the people of this town didn't want
               Pinocchio to be leader. We couldn't understand
               his language. He was different from us.

Bailey: Pinocchio was our saviour.

Barnum: A soul mate.

Bailey   A kindred spirit. Even if he did lead us up the
               garden path.

Scrooge: The book is just full of mischief.

Pinocchio: You didn't like what Diablo wrote. Because he
               wrote the truth. So you sent him away.
               You didn't let anyone else into the toon who
               spoke his language.

Who spoke my language.
Until now.

Bailey: We thought this would be a safe place.

Barnum: We left our homes because we were told they
                   never wanted to hear from us again and said
                   good riddance.

Conrad: We escaped riddles of debt.

Bailey: We had exhausted all our job options.

Barnum: Diablo's book said this was a toon of
                   opportunities.

Conrad: Scrooge you must learn how to read the book.

Barnum: We can each teach you a section of the book.

Bailey: From the basics.

Conrad: Learn our language.

Bailey: The text reading backwards can be taught by me.

Barnum: The text in numbers can be taught be me as it
                   reads like ingredients.

Conrad: The text written by a squiggly hand can be
                   taught by me.

Scrooge: How can I possibly learn a stream of
                   consciousness? I do not understand it.

Pinocchio:	It is the native language of the town which was nearly lost.
Bailey:	It's written like magic.
Barnum:	We will alter the town's attitudes from the roots.
Pinocchio:	It did have good prospects once upon a time.
Bailey:	But it wasn't led properly.
Conrad:	The book tells us how to lead.
Barnum:	Put us in charge.
Bailey:	Let us cut and serve meat.
Barnum:	Bake and serve bread.
Conrad:	Make and sell candles.
Pinocchio:	I am the heir to this toon and I pledge to sign and hand the toon over to Barnum, Bailey and Conrad who will teach their skills and language to others like Diablo wanted.

Beat

So Scrooge helped Old Mother Hubbard break free from the cupboard. He studied Diablo's words like a scholar with Barnum, Bailey and Conrad guided him like mentors. The language became identified with the toon and the gates swung open where Pinocchio welcomed everyone.